"TELL THE CHRISTIANS IN THE WEST ABOUT OUR VICTORIES and our problems as believers here in the Soviet Union. The more people know there—the easier it is for us here." So speaks Fyodr, a Soviet Christian who can take neither his life nor his faith for granted. He is only one of the voices you will hear in this cry from the soul of a spiritually oppressed people.

"I understand sadness," said Galya, a Russian college student who spoke of Christ to missionaries Anita and Peter Deyneka, Jr. Then she disappeared. In a protestant church attended by a surprising number of youths, the Deynekas meet a young couple who came out of curiosity and left changed forever. Gregori, cautious on the street of Leningrad's busy Nevsky Prospekt, is only too happy to accept a Bible in the shadows of a nearby street. Steffan and Vasily, leaders in the church, want a Bible at any cost. Courageous Christians Mikhail and Anna risk arrest holding church meetings in their home.

Come and meet the Russians as the Deynekas did. You will never forget them.

CHRISTIANS IN THE SHADOW OF THE KREMLIN

Anita and Peter Deyneka, Jr.

David C. Cook Publishing Co.

850 NORTH GROVE AVENUE • ELGIN, IL 60120

In Canada: David C. Cook Publishing (Canada) Ltd., Weston, Ontario M9L 1T4

David C. Cook Publishing Co., Elgin, IL 60120

Printed in the United States of America
Library of Congress Catalog Number: 74-17730
ISBN: 0-912692-48-0

CONTENTS

Foreword

More than 57 years have elapsed since the revolution which brought communism to power in Russia. That mighty upheaval transformed the Russian nation, setting in motion forces that have affected the course of history.

Christians especially have witnessed events in the Soviet Union with foreboding. Dialectical materialism sought to rule out the supernatural. Religion was subjected to ridicule, oppression and rigid restriction.

Has half a century of suppression erased all remnants of religion?

Anita and Peter Deyneka have given us a firsthand glimpse of life in Russia through these gripping accounts of their personal contacts. It makes thrilling reading.

The Deynekas found deep interest and spiritual hunger even in students and workers who have been shielded from any exposure to Christian influences. The state has failed to eradicate an interest in the supernatural—confirming again the observation that man is incurably religious!

That state of affairs is not entirely surprising when one recalls that Svetlana Stalin, daughter of the former Soviet head of state Joseph Stalin, stated: "I was brought up in a family where there was never any talk about God. However, I found that it was impossible to exist without God in one's heart."

Then there is the more recent case of Aleksandr Solzhenitsyn. Born near the time of the revolution and having lived his entire life in the Soviet Union, he should have been the epitome of a society which has no place for God.

Not so. Solzhenitsyn, a brave symbol of the human spirit in rebellion against crass ideological materialism, has said, "I myself see Christianity today as the only living spiritual force capable of undertaking the spiritual healing of Russia."

The Deynekas encountered ordinary people who were dissatisfied with a one-dimensional view of life. It is thrilling to think that there are many others in Russia who are restless in spirit and open to the Gospel.

The section of the book dealing with Christians in Russia—your and my spiritual brothers and sisters—is especially moving. Here we encounter choice spirits—the type of which this world is not worthy. They are Christians whose testimonies have an apostolic radiance and whose lives are given over to the Lord Jesus Christ.

The reading of this book thrilled me and made me sense anew that Jesus Christ is very much alive and at work in all corners of His world.

Charlotte, North Carolina   LEIGHTON FORD

Preface

The young Russian hunched forward, his voice a whisper. "Do people there really know how it is with us here? Are they praying for us?"

During our extensive travels inside the U.S.S.R., we have heard those same questions repeated many times. This is one of the reasons we wrote this book.

Many Russians who live behind the U.S.S.R.'s guarded borders would like to know the citizens of the rest of the world better. They wish we knew more about their lives.

We discovered that Christians especially yearn for contact with fellow believers from other countries. But the formidable barbed-wire border stretching from the Baltic to the Black Sea that Winston Churchill called the "Iron Curtain" effectively clamps off meaningful contact with the outside.

Because of their circumscribed situation, Russian Christians feel a deep bond with believers in the West who send shortwave radio programs into their country. These Gospel broadcasts, which are transmitted daily from several missionary stations, become a spiritual lifeline to believers who are treated as aliens in their avowedly atheistic country.

Russian believers who cannot buy a Bible or Christian book in any bookstore in their own country are also grateful for Christians in the West who haven't forgotten them.

As the encounters in this book illustrate, many non-

Christians are equally eager to read God's Word. This spiritual search is startling in a country where every Russian child is instructed in the Soviet schools to be an atheist.

Since the Bolshevik Revolution, a generation of Russians has been reared to believe that ". . . both Moses and Jesus are mythical characters" (*The Unabridged Soviet Encyclopedia,* Volume 5, p. 157).

In this book, which is a series of personal encounters with Soviet students, workers, and Christians, we have tried to let the people whom we met speak for themselves.

In all instances names of people in this book have been changed. In some cases we have changed or abbreviated the names of places. But the encounters are true and the people real.

We wish you could have met these Russians and experienced their friendliness and openhearted generosity. Travel to the U.S.S.R. has been encouraged recently by the Soviet government, and last year three million tourists from all over the world visited Russia. As you read this book, we hope you also will want to visit the people of the U.S.S.R.

Chicago, Illinois   ANITA AND PETER DEYNEKA, JR.

THE STUDENTS

"Aren't All Educated People Atheists?"

Momentarily, we wondered if we had the wrong address. Then we saw rows of people ringed around the narrow porch because they couldn't crowd inside the wooden house. We knew we had found the Baptist Church —the only Protestant church in M., a city with a population of 600,000.

We tried to stand inconspicuously among the overflowing congregation on the porch, but we were soon identified as visitors. A path opened through the people, and two beaming babushkas led us insistently to chairs which were vacated for us in the front row.

From our seat, which faced the congregation, I counted the young people. Amazingly, there were at least a hundred—a startling percentage where youth under eighteen are officially discouraged and often threatened if they attend Christian gatherings, according to such laws as the Soviet government's 1966 decree on church life.

A youth orchestra, squeezed in front of the pulpit,

played a song they had composed themselves. A choir standing behind them sang the haunting words, "If we never meet again on earth, we will meet in Heaven. . . ."

Three small children leaned against a decrepit pump organ propped near the choir. Between songs the wrinkled grandmother who played the organ crowded the children beside her on the bench. A little girl with a fluffy white ribbon woven in her long braids huddled next to the old organist and gazed soberly at us visitors.

We discovered we were not the only visitors that Sunday afternoon at the church in M. Seated beside us was an American woman we had seen earlier at our hotel. A young Russian student couple sat uneasily beside her.

"How did you find the church?" Anita whispered to the American woman.

The woman motioned to the young couple sitting stiffly beside her. "I met them on the bus and I asked them for directions. They guided me all the way to the church and I invited them to stay."

I studied the young couple. The boy glanced furtively at the congregation. The girl sat nervously at his side. She was the only woman in the congregation who wore slacks.

Three lay pastors had already preached and the choir had sung several minor hymns from a few shared hand-written hymnals. Then an old man with an unruly beard, who was one of the lay preachers, walked unsteadily down from the platform to where we sat beside the American woman and the young Russian couple.

In a loud whisper, the pastor greeted us visitors. The young couple shrank back in their chairs.

Then the pastor asked my name. "Ah, but you must bring us greetings!" he exclaimed when I told him.

By now I understood that the pastor was asking me to preach. Once in a Russian church I had questioned the pastor, "What kind of greetings?"

He had replied with a smile, "Greetings from Paul, and

16

Luke and John—the kind of greetings that will cause people to repent!"

When I came to the pulpit, I first greeted the congregation in traditional Russian fashion—from my parents, from the other radio missionaries, and from Christians in America.

The faces of the congregation lit in recognition when I mentioned the radio missionaries. They all stood except the young couple who seemed uncertain what they should do.

"*Preevet, preevet*—greetings," the congregation replied in unison in the customary way, but with a fervent warmth that communicated the brotherhood Russian believers feel toward Christians living beyond the confining borders of the Soviet Union.

Then I brought "greetings" from the Bible. I spoke from I John 1 about the certainty of eternal life beyond the grave. The congregation punctuated my sermon with nods of agreement. "*Da pravda*—yes, that is true," a bent grandmother sitting behind the young Russian couple agreed loudly.

The two young Russians had not relaxed, but they listened intently to the sermon. Questions flickered in the boy's eyes. I hoped I would be able to meet him after the service.

After the last prayer the congregation surged around us visitors. Bouquets of chrysanthemums appeared mysteriously, and the friendly young Christians shoved them into our hands.

Tanya, a pretty music teacher with wavy black hair and shining eyes, greeted the young couple visiting her church and showed them a photo. "Our youth group," she said proudly.

Tanya wanted to talk to Anita, but in the crowd privacy was impossible. "Could you come back on the bus with us?" Anita asked. Tanya nodded eagerly, but then she glanced for approval to an older woman standing beside her. The older woman said nothing, but her expression was apprehensive, and Tanya's eagerness faded.

Over the commotion I heard one of the lay pastors urge the enthusiastic young Christians, "Please, brothers and sisters, let's have order." Some of the young people produced cameras. "Please—only take photos inside the church," the pastor prodded cautiously.

However, when we were finally able to edge out of the church, the zealous young photographers quickly ushered us all into a group by the church gate. The young Russian couple who had accompanied the American woman were pulled into the picture. Their expressions wavered between curiosity and fear.

We clutched our flowers tensely. We saw the fearful expressions of the lay pastors, and we were afraid to stay. But we hesitated to leave abruptly and offend the enthusiastic young Christians, who insisted they must take one more photo to "remember the Sunday when we were all together."

A taxi bumped down the unpaved road. The driver slowed to stare with unconcealed curiosity at the joyful crowd in front of the church. Sadly, we detached ourselves from the young Christians.

Tanya was nowhere in sight. But the American woman and the young Russian couple who had shown her to the church followed after us.

Several of the Christians accompanied us up the main street to the bus stop. They embraced us and helped shove us into the bulging bus. They waved good-bye with white handkerchiefs as the bus lurched away down the street.

The young couple, whom I still hadn't met, caught the same bus and pushed toward the front. I wished we could meet them, but I saw no way to hurdle the layers of passengers between us.

Finally the bus throttled to a stop near our hotel. The

American woman stepped off and so did the young couple. "They want to talk to you about what you said in your sermon," the American woman explained when we were a discreet distance from other pedestrians.

By now we were near the Intourist hotel. "*Loochye*—it is best if we part now and meet again in the park," the Russian boy suggested.

The park was already draped in dark, but not deserted. Despite the frigid fall air, people strolled leisurely along graceful paths beside the splendid gardens shrouded with moonlight.

The young Russian introduced himself as Volodya, and gestured to the girl, "my friend, Sonya."

The two Russians were students at the university in the city of M. They had never been to a church service or met a Christian before that Sunday.

"There were so many young people at the meeting!" Sonya exclaimed.

"At the university they told us only old people attended," Volodya mused.

Sonya volunteered that she had always had "an interest in religious things." Among many of her friends she confided it was "fashionable to own a cross or an icon."

"Of course, I am a Komsomol (Young Communist League) member," Volodya proudly said at the outset. "I know that we are supposed to have nothing to do with Christians," he paused in bewilderment, "but your words at the church pierced my heart. I decided I must talk to you. Is it really possible there is a God? Can there really be life after death? . . ." His questions tumbled out.

"My parents are atheists. Of course, I was raised as an atheist," Volodya explained. As we circled the paths in the park, Volodya recalled his university lessons in atheism. "Could God create a place where He could not go?" His professor in atheism class insisted that this question itself proves the nonexistence of God.

19

"Are all your professors atheists?" I asked.

"But, of course," he replied. "Aren't all educated people?"

I told Volodya about the Christian college I had attended "where all of the professors believe in God."

"Were they real professors?" Volodya was skeptical.

When I confirmed they were and that many of them had earned doctor's degrees, the young Russian was aghast.

For a long time we discussed Christianity from a scientific perspective. "Truth," Volodya's professors had embedded in his mind "is synonymous with science."

He was incredulous when I told him about archaeological discoveries that support the historical authenticity of the Bible. He had never heard that historians recorded the existence of Jesus Christ. In the official Soviet encyclopedia he had read that "Jesus was a myth."

For an hour and a half more we walked in the cold dark park and talked. Volodya hunched into his thin coat and trudged meditatively beside me.

"Such an important decision," I urged him, "should not be decided for you by the Komsomol, by your professors, or by anyone else. You should read Jesus' words and decide for yourself."

"But where will I get a Bible?" Volodya abruptly turned to his girl friend who had said earlier that she had once read some verses from the Bible. "*Eemeyesh Bibliyu*—do you have a Bible?" he asked her urgently.

Sonya didn't own a Bible herself, but she had once borrowed one to read. "Sometimes," she said hesitantly, "it is possible to buy a Bible on the black market—but they can cost a month's wages. It is more than I can afford."

"Is it legal for you to have a Bible?" I asked the young couple. They consulted briefly and decided it must not be unlawful since they had heard that a few Bibles had once been printed in the Soviet Union. "Our own government

20

wouldn't print any book that was illegal," Sonya reasoned.

"*Podarok*—a gift to you from Christians in the West," I said as I slipped Volodya a Russian New Testament I carried in my pocket.

Flickering shadows from the eternal flame of a nearby World War II monument fell across our path and lit the faces of the two young Russians as they walked away with a new light.

A Little Celebration

We knew there was something different about our driver as soon as we climbed into his taxi.

Like other Russian drivers, he drove with abandon, making it a point to compete with the few vehicles on the wide highway. He used his clutch freely and conserved gas by turning off the ignition and coasting whenever possible.

The young driver, who wore a jaunty beret, also shared the Russian passion for fresh air. I saw Anita inch away from the blast of October night air pouring through his half-open taxicab window.

But this young driver was unlike any other taxi driver we had encountered so far in Russia. He smiled and even laughed with a girl who sat in the front seat beside him. For us, a jovial taxi driver was a new experience.

I remembered the sullen driver in another Russian city whose face I had never seen clearly and who seemed welded to the steering wheel. He also overcharged me.

Or there was the brusque driver in Moscow who rudely agreed to "try to find" the Baptist Church—assuring us he had no maps, which for security reasons often are not available in the Soviet Union. The Moscow driver warned us that he would probably "have to drive around extra" to locate the church.

In lieu of a map, he hollered at passersby, demanding— not asking—directions. With embarrassment, I recalled how he had screeched the taxi up to a sidewalk and screamed at a helpless, hunched *babushka,* "Woman, tell me where this street is!" She didn't know, and with a curse for her efforts, the driver sped away.

As I studied the amiable young taxi driver in front of us, chatting with the girl, I was also surprised to notice that he made no effort to eavesdrop as Anita and I talked. Many taxi drivers I had met in Russia listened closely— even if the conversation was in English.

The driver and the girl were laughing merrily when he remarked in Russian, half to her, and seemingly half to us, "I guess you know we've been having a little celebration here." He motioned with a twist of his neck to another of the innumerable posters we had seen all over the Soviet Union announcing the anniversary of Lenin's hundredth birthday.

When I conceded cautiously that we had noticed a few signs, he laughed. "Is it possible you could have *not* noticed them?

"So you speak Russian?" Yuri said when we had talked awhile. "You have a pretty good vocabulary," he added wryly.

"Not really," I said modestly. "My vocabulary is very limited because I don't use Russian every day. You probably know several thousand more words than I because you live here."

"Oh, I wouldn't say that," the driver replied with the same mischievous laugh. "Even Vladimir only knew ten thousand words, they say—and that was including the foreign ones!" By Vladimir I understood the young Russian meant Vladimir Ilych Lenin, the father of Russian communism.

However, I was too startled to reply to his witticism, which by Soviet standards was almost risque. I had never heard a Soviet citizen—especially when there was more than one person listening—speak in anything but respectful tones about Lenin.

I remembered the official tour of the city we had taken that morning with two Intourist guides. Luba, the chief guide, was training a younger guide, Svetlana. As we drove under one of the ubiquitous Lenin banners blazoned across the street, Luba announced reverently, "All progressive peoples are now celebrating the hundredth anniversary of Lenin's birthday."

That morning under Luba's determined tutelage, we saw numerous statues of Lenin and we learned how many meters high most of them were. The highest one, we were told, had been erected at "the insistence of university students who also volunteered to do the construction."

The taxi passed some exquisite domed Orthodox churches, with little comment from Luba. When we asked, we discovered the churches were usually "museums of the people" or public works buildings. A pathetic few were "working churches—or churches open for worship."

From the same tour we learned how many pairs of shoes a city factory produces monthly and how many bushels of grain were hauled from the surrounding farmlands each week to the city. However, beyond their cautiously programmed comments, we never did learn much about Luba or Svetlana.

From previous visits we knew that most Soviet citizens consider chewing gum a treat since they cannot buy it in their own country. Anita offered each of the girls a piece of gum.

Svetlana waited to see if her superior, Luba, would accept. Luba did not want to offend us, but was also wary about compromising her communist principles.

Finally, she gingerly accepted the gum with the strange explanation that "Soviet people do not especially care about gum. It is not," she explained dutifully, "that the Soviet government is opposed to gum. In fact, we are considering possibly manufacturing it." From that circuitous explanation, we inferred that capitalist gum—though it is not a necessity—may one day be produced in the U.S.S.R.

If such an innocuous item as a piece of gum was a possible point of heresy, the young taxi driver's badinage about Lenin seemed, to my Soviet-acclimated mind, close to blasphemy.

Changing the subject from Lenin's vocabulary, the taxi driver introduced himself as Yuri Pavlovich. Jerking a nod toward us, he asked abruptly, "Are you married?" We said we were and introduced ourselves.

"Are you married?" I asked Yuri.

"No," he replied and leaning over to the girl, teased, "Will you marry me?" With a laugh, he introduced us to his girl friend, Nadya.

Pursuing the joke, I said lightly, "I could marry you right now. I'm a minister."

Yuri suddenly grew sober. Solemnly he asked, "Why are you a minister? Isn't it all just a fairy tale? Do you really think there is a God?"

As we talked, I learned that Yuri had only contacted Christianity through courses on religion and atheism at the local university, where both he and his girl friend studied. He equated religion with a grotesque life-size display of the Spanish Inquisition that he remembered seeing once when he had visited the Museum of Religion and Atheism in Leningrad.

"A lot of harm has been done in the name of religion," I

agreed as we drove through the darkness. "But Christ and religion are not the same. Jesus came to earth to give us life, not religion. Christ, Himself, said that He is Life."

I told Yuri and Nadya the story of Nicodemus who came to Christ by night. Yuri slowed the taxi and listened intently. When I came to the part of the story where Christ tells Nicodemus he must be born again, Yuri interrupted explosively, "But is it possible? How can I be born again?"

By this time we were almost to our hotel. Yuri was undisguisedly interested in our discussion. His taxi was crawling and I knew he wanted to continue our conversation—but how?

"Why don't we just drive around and see some more of your city," I said casually, deciding that the extra expense was worth the chance to tell the two young Russians more about Jesus Christ.

As we drove around the city, the two students listened hungrily to my explanation of Christianity. "A man's life is not complete without Christ," I said.

When I paused, Yuri objected thoughtfully, "But Pyotr Petrovich, I am an economics student. I know you Americans care only for business and personal gain. We Soviets fought together against the fascists. Now we are sacrificing and working together to build a country—a society. For a Soviet man that is enough in life," he concluded without much conviction.

"Your people have suffered, but it's amazing the way you have rebuilt your country," I sympathized.

Satisfied that my answer was not defensive, Yuri ventured further. Had I read Lenin and Marx? Did I still believe what Jesus taught?

Since he had never had the opportunity to read the Bible or freely investigate any other philosophy besides communism, Yuri was at first suspicious, but envious when I told him I had read writings of Lenin and Marx.

26

After another forty-five minutes of spirited discussion we neared the hotel again. Yuri pulled to the curb about fifty yards from the hotel and shut off the motor and headlights.

I knew it wasn't safe for the two young Russians to be sitting talking amicably with us foreigners—even fifty yard from the hotel. I wished there were some place—any place—in that Ukrainian city where we could talk freely that night.

"You've read Marx and Lenin—would you like to read what Jesus says?" I asked the two university students.

They reached eagerly for the *Gospels of John and Mark* in the Russian language that I held out for them. As I handed the booklets across the seat, I noticed a man who had been standing suspiciously long in the shadows in front of our hotel, watching our parked car. He turned toward the cab. Nadya and Yuri, in the front seat, were turned toward us. They didn't see the stranger approaching from behind.

Nadya, who had been quietly considering the conversation, turned and spoke to Anita, "And you—are you also a Christian? Have you been born again?"

By this time the observer was near the taxi, staring at us through the darkness. Quietly, I warned Nadya and Yuri about the approaching man. We didn't need to explain. They were Russians. They understood. They thanked us for the Gospels and sped off into the night.

"I Never Felt That Way Before"

The Friday Anita and I met Galya, a gray October haze hung over Moscow that shrouded even the gold Kremlin dome.

We decided to spend the afternoon at the Tretyakov Art Gallery—the magnificent museum of Russian art in Moscow. Despite the rain, the museum was crowded.

We first met Galya, a young girl about college age, in the basement of the museum. She was wearing a three-cornered red paper hat—a souvenir, she told us later, that she bought at a patriotic festival that day.

Galya listened with unconcealed curiosity when I spoke in Russian and asked a stiff guard for directions to the paintings of Ilya Repin, a famous Soviet artist who was a neighbor of Leo Tolstoy.

When we finished speaking with the guard, Galya smiled shyly at Anita and stepped toward us. "Are you tourists?" she asked timidly. "Have you visited the Pushkin Art

Museum yet? They have an excellent collection of impressionist paintings."

Galya loved art, and her black, smiling eyes brimmed with excitement when she spoke of paintings she had seen in Moscow's museums. "I do not understand your American abstract art," she admitted, "but I am curious."

Galya admired the style of Soviet realism. She pointed to a tall painting before us in black and gray that depicted a crew of sooty coal miners descending to a pit. "That painting makes me sad—but I understand the sadness," she said.

Two hours later when the museum guards were solemnly shaking small bells to warn visitors that the museum was closing, we met Galya again.

"Zdravstvooyte—hello again," we greeted her in Russian. With sudden generosity Galya unclasped a small pin she was wearing commemorating the fourteenth anniversary of the Soviet "Liberation of Hungary." She insisted that Anita must keep the pin as a "souvenir of our friendship."

The guards, impatient to close the museum, shooed us toward the door, but Galya wanted to talk. "Would you like to walk to the subway with us?" Anita invited.

In the obscurity of the dark, drizzly street, the young Russian girl with black cropped hair told us she was from a town of ten thousand people in the Ural Mountains—the craggy divide which separates European Russia from Siberia.

An architectural student, Galya had traveled five thousand miles from her Siberian home with a group of other students on a tour to Moscow sponsored by the Komsomol (Communist Youth League), to which she belonged at her university.

Galya had never been farther from her home than Moscow, and she was elated by her trip to the capital city. She was a tourist—seeing the sights, collecting souvenirs, eager to tell her friends at home about her trip. Proudly she showed us a packet of post cards she had bought with bright photos of Moscow.

The conversation turned to our travels. "Was it difficult for you to come to our country?" Galya asked. "How long did you have to wait for your passport? Have you traveled in other countries?"

When I told her that I had traveled in many parts of the world, Galya sighed softly. "We could never travel so freely," she observed.

"What did you study in your university?" Galya wanted to know. When I told her Bible literature, she was curious. "I have heard of the Bible, but have never read it. In our country it's difficult to buy a Bible," she sighed.

I wondered if Galya had never met a Russian believer. "Have you heard of the Baptists?" I ventured. (In Russia, almost all Russian Protestant Christians are called Baptists.)

Galya hesitated. When she did reply, she framed her words to spare our feelings. She had heard of the Baptists, but only at school where her teachers ridiculed them.

"I do know a little about God," Galya stammered shyly as if she were sharing a secret. "Twice I went to an Orthodox Church on my own—once in my home town and once when I was away visiting my aunt in another city. But my mother and father found out. They are Communist Party members. They were furious and told me that I would disgrace them if I ever went to church again.

"When I was at church," Galya stopped to search for words, "I felt something different. I felt as though I was finding myself—I never felt that way before. I wish I could go again."

"Maybe you felt God's Spirit inside the church," I suggested after we had walked several steps in silence on the leaf strewn streets.

"I do not understand myself." Galya shrugged her

31

shoulders, ruefully. She paused beside a black and white birch tree. "Here I am—a member of the Komsomol, and wanting to go to church."

The subway could not have been more than a mile at the most from the museum, but after we had prolonged our walk an hour in that direction so we could talk, Galya still hung back. She had more questions to ask about Christianity.

"I wish I could read the words of Jesus myself," she said wistfully. I didn't have a Bible with me, but I did have two paperback copies of Luke's and John's Gospels. I handed them to Galya. She thanked me and slipped them into her pocket to shield them from the mist. By now Galya's red paper hat was flat and wet, and the three of us were shivering. "I'll ride along with you in the direction of your hotel," she volunteered when we finally reached the subway stop.

The elegant subway had been suffocatingly crowded when we had ridden to the museum. Now it was nearly empty. The three of us walked in silent admiration past the chandeliers, marble walls, and magnificent frescoes which decorate Moscow's subway.

It was 10:30 by the time we finally neared our hotel. We trudged under a towering statue of Lenin. "What do you think of our leader, Lenin?" she asked abruptly.

"I respect many leaders in my country," I replied vaguely, "and I suppose you respect your leaders."

"Yes," she agreed fervently. "I respect Lenin, but it is more than that. Lenin is the savior of Russia. He's like a brother to me!"

Galya wanted us to meet her again the following night—Saturday. We had planned to go to church. I knew there would be young people at the meeting. We wondered if Galya would like to come along. "I would love to," she agreed impulsively.

Galya thanked us for the Bible. She shook my hand and

hugged Anita. "Until tomorrow night," were Galya's last words as she slipped into the darkness.

Saturday night we waited for two hours where we had planned to meet—but Galya never came. We never saw her again.

A Vicious Circle

The stately prerevolutionary hotel where Intourist assigned us to stay in Leningrad stands near the city's main boulevard—Nevsky Prospekt. Like so much of majestic Leningrad—the capital of Russia from Czar Peter the Great to the time of the Bolshevik Revolution—the old hotel is a genteel reminder of Russia's aristocratic past.

We walked down the hotel's graceful marble stairs from our room on the fifth floor to the Intourist bureau on the first floor, and were swiftly transported from the world of prerevolutionary grandeur to the realities of Russian socialism.

Inside the Intourist bureau, the official Russian tourist agency, a portrait of Lenin peered from the wall. Yellowing curtains sagged from the windows. A woman clerk in a severe blue uniform with a high bun of hair pulled painfully back from her face presided indifferently at the Intourist counter that handled meal coupons.

A Russian tourist who needed directions to the proper counter edged meekly to the front of the short line of foreign tourists. "Shut up and stay in line if you have a question," the woman rasped grimly, her eyes fixed on the papers before her.

Finally we reached the counter and obtained our meal coupons—without once seeing a full view of the woman's face.

Inside the dining room, we sat by a retired American couple who visited a different country every year. They had read about Leningrad in *National Geographic* magazine and were rapturous about Russia.

A young Russian in a black turtleneck sweater and modishly long hair sauntered to our table. He seated himself nonchalantly and casually smoked a succession of cigarettes while he surveyed the four of us Americans.

"Leningrad is a beautiful city—*kraseeveey gorod*," Anita tried to open the conversation.

"Maybe you'd like to come live here," he responded dourly.

When the waitress brought his borscht, the young Russian shoved aside his cigarette and reached for pepper which he shook vigorously into the already-seasoned soup. "I like strong things. After all, what else is there to live for?"

He seemed to relax with the first spoonful of borscht, and was soon telling us his name was Viktor and that he liked to visit the restaurant in the grand old hotel as often as he could afford. "That," he complained, "is seldom." He had come to the restaurant that night "because my wife is at her mother's home in Moscow having a baby—and I don't like to cook."

Viktor finished his borscht and ordered vodka. He sipped it slowly and turned expansively talkative. "I'm in the university—here in Leningrad. I am a so-called student of journalism," he replied bitterly when I asked him

36

about his work.

"So-called?" I repeated.

"Ha, it's a joke," he sneered. "How can we be journalists in this country? Here I am . . . supposed to learn how to write the news . . . but I can't write what I feel. I'm not even allowed to leave the country to find out what's really happening in the world!" he exploded.

Viktor's voice rose incautiously, "The only great writers that we have are Pasternak, Bulgakov, and Solzhenitsyn." He lowered his voice, "Thank God the censors have decided that Tolstoy was a communist at heart. At least we can read him!"

Melancholy strains of the Russian ballad "Katyusha" floated down from the elegant, expensive dining room up the hall. "I wish I could afford to eat in there," Viktor gestured glumly to the upper dining room. He consoled himself with another gulp of clear vodka.

The American couple at the other end of the table tried to inject a cultural question about Leningrad's Hermitage Museum into our Russian conversation. I translated their question, but the young journalist rudely ignored them and pounded his fist near the vodka bottle.

"I tell you, Pyotr Petrovich," he growled, "the whole thing is a vicious circle. There is no way out. And what use is there trying to fix the fringe? We can't change. If I don't write what I'm told, I don't get an apartment—or I just won't get a job. I have to have an apartment. My wife is having a baby," he repeated glumly.

At that moment, a girl in a flowing blue chiffon dress floated over to our table. I realized she must have come from the dining room up the hall. She laid her hand on Viktor's shoulder and bent to whisper to him. Her long flaxen hair fell into his face.

"Later, afterwards . . ." I heard Viktor reply, and the girl swept back into the ballroom.

"Just an old friend of mine," Viktor poured himself

another drink indifferently. "She plays the harp in the orchestra."

By this time Viktor was smoking again. His attention suddenly swerved to the American couple sitting across the table. "Those Americans," he surveyed them shrewdly. "Do you think they would do a little favor for me?"

Viktor asked me to translate his proposal for a "little transaction" to the Americans.

He wanted the American couple to buy him one carton of cigarettes at Beriozka—the Intourist store with special consumer goods which can be purchased only with foreign currency. He proposed to pay them roubles in exchange for the dollars they spent.

"I love foreign cigarettes—ours taste like sawdust," Viktor complained.

I translated Viktor's request to the Americans who were pleased to participate in what they seemed to consider an act of international good will. "It's like hands across the ocean!" the woman exclaimed.

The Americans scurried down to the Beriozka store to buy Viktor's cigarettes, and the young Russian leaned back with satisfaction. "Vodka . . . cigarettes . . . women," he winked, "what else has meaning in life?"

When I replied that Jesus Christ the Son of God had given meaning in my life, Viktor was skeptical about the "religious words." But like most Russians he was eager for a philosophical discussion.

Was Christianity "really important in my life," he probed, or was I "just pretending"? If I genuinely believed in God, how could I be sure that "He really existed"?

I told Viktor about the Bible—the book where he could read God's words for himself. He reflected soberly when I spoke of God's Word, but when I mentioned the word "*Bibliyu*," a gleam of recognition fluttered in his eyes.

He leaned forward conspiratorily, "Do you have any Bibles, Pyotr Petrovich? Listen, if you have a Bible, I will pay you well. Frankly," he phrased his request carefully, "I know several people who are interested in philosophy. Please, if you have a Bible, or more than one—sell them to me. I can make us a good profit. You can do me a great favor!"

Viktor's pleasure at the prospect of making profit from the Bibles was so intense, that he wilted noticeably when I told him the Bibles I had brought along to Russia weren't for sale—they were gifts for people searching for God's Word.

However, he shrugged with goodnatured resignation at my firm explanation and did not try to barter any further for the Bibles.

By this time, the Americans had returned with Viktor's cigarettes. "Those rich Americans. Their lives are as useless as mine," he nodded toward the retired couple when they were leaving the dining room. "What meaning are they living for?"

For almost an hour longer, Anita and I sat at the restaurant table with Viktor, discussing meaning in life. I talked about the meaning of Christianity to Viktor, who was in no hurry and seemingly heedless to the risk of extended conversations with foreigners.

By the end of our conversation, I realized that Viktor's interest in Christianity was sincere, and I wished I could leave him a Bible.

At the last minute, I decided to give Viktor a booklet of the *Gospel of Mark* that I had in my pocket.

"*Spaceebo, spaceebo*—thank you," he beamed.

The girl in the blue chiffon dress appeared again in the doorway and beckoned to Viktor. "Well, Pyotr Petrovich, I have to go," he mumbled. The *Gospel of Mark* in his pocket, he disappeared through the door.

THE WORKERS

You Can't Move Two Mountains

"Look what Hitler did. And he came in the name of God!" the Russian said with a clinching smile. Sure that he had posed an unanswerable argument, Dimitri slowly sipped his vodka. I studied his bloodshot eyes and couldn't decide if he really wanted an answer, or if he was only hoping for the diversion of an argument.

We had just met Dimitri for the first time only an hour before. It was nine at night. We had come into an almost deserted cafe for some supper that we had not had time to eat before a church meeting earlier that night.

There were few customers and plenty of waitresses at nine o'clock. Optimistically we thought that a quick supper might be possible. From previous encounters in Russian restaurants, we had learned that anywhere from one to two hours is normal waiting time and beyond two hours was not unheard of.

We had already met more than one frustrated tourist

who was spending four to six hours a day waiting inside restaurants—a delay that we suspected did not unduly displease harried Intourist government guides who have difficulty enough keeping track of tourists.

Most of the tables were empty and we chose one by the door. If we wanted to be served, we would have to move to "an empty table in another section," a stout young waitress snapped. We did and a few minutes later, a hastily-shaven Russian citizen was also shown to our table.

We greeted the disheveled Russian with a smile as he sat down at our small table. Since we still had not been served, we watched with interest as the man pressed something into the willing waitress' hand and was served with polite speed. We surmised that tipping—which we had read in tourist guide books is an insult to a communist worker—is not invariably unwelcome.

We wanted to talk with the Russian now enjoying his vodka and open-faced sausage sandwiches, but we hesitated to speak first. Most Russians we had met in restaurants were warm and friendly, but a few were obviously frightened. The Russian sitting beside us now lit a cigarette and asked if we minded if he smoked.

"Not at all," I replied, glad for a conversation opener. He extended a hand across to our still unserved side of the table and introduced himself as Dimitri Ivanovich.

With another wink and some more kopecks for the waitress, he ordered more vodka. I studied Dimitri Ivanovich. His eyes were blurred—his face cynical and calculating but at the same time congenial.

We exchanged the usual comments about the weather and our work. It was when I said I was a preacher that he changed. "You Christians—how can you talk about God? Look what Hitler did, and he came in the name of God."

His voice was cold. "Did you know that every soldier in the German army had 'in the name of God' inscribed on his belt buckle! How do you explain that, Pyotr Petrovich?"

With mercurial Russian charm, Dimitri's bitterness suddenly brightened to a smile. He poured himself another drink of vodka and waited.

I understood his anger at Hitler's atrocities. "But, there is a difference," I explained, "between people who say they are religious and people who are true followers of Christ."

I told Dimitri about my own conversion to Christ. He was skeptical but listened thoughtfully. "Christ changed my life," I said. I talked about God's love that sent His own Son to die for man. Dimitri's smile mocked, but his eyes softened.

"Well, Pyotr Petrovich," he volunteered with sudden magnanimity, "it may be true for you what you are saying, but I am a communist, and I am an atheist. I was raised right through the Komsomol and I never had time for religion."

"What did you do after you left school?" I asked.

He rolled up a sweaty shirt sleeve to a wild tattoo on his arm. "I served twelve years in the Soviet navy."

"Did you ever hear any of the Christian radio programs from outside your country?"

"Yes, yes, of course I've heard," Dimitri smiled. "Almost everybody here listens sometimes to your American programs, but don't let that fool you.

"We communists have a saying—peace, joy and brotherhood—that's all we want. Yet look what war has done to us. Hitler came with a cross and look what he did to us," he chanted. "It may be true what you say for yourself, Pyotr Petrovich," he conceded, "but you can't change the faith of a nation. Anyway, it doesn't make sense. Why would a man like Christ come and die for other people?"

"To give peace and forgiveness on earth, and life after death to people like you and me," I replied.

"I am a simple man with an open Russian heart," Dimitri insisted. "I understand what you are trying to say, but I can't agree. It's strange meeting you, Pyotr Petrovich," he shrugged. "My mother was just like you. All her life she tried to teach me to believe in God."

He finished his sandwiches and gulped several more glasses of vodka. He shook my hand with the grasp of a friend and his clouded eyes searched my face. "When you think of me, Pyotr Petrovich, remember the Russian proverb, 'You can't move two mountains . . . but two people can come together.' "

"Could You Give Me That Little Book?"

When we first met Lena, she was cleaning hotel rooms in the city of N. in northern Russia. Later Lena told us she was born in Finland but had lived most of her life in Leningrad before she moved to the city of N.

Like all tourists, when we arrived at the city of N., we were met at the airport by an Intourist representative who took us to our hotel—a destination unknown to us. For security reasons, Intourist does not usually notify tourists ahead of time which hotel they may expect to stay in.

When we arrived at the hotel—which happened to be the only one in the City of N.—room 205 was not ready. It was late fall and the hotel did not look overcrowded. "Would it be possible to switch to another room that is ready?" we asked the stern clerk at the front desk.

"*Nyet, nyet,*" she replied adamantly. "I have instructions that you are to stay in room 205. That room is being prepared for you," she insisted with a finality that left us

48

Some Christian parents bring their children to church despite official atheism. This Russian boy sits under a plaque that declares, "God is love."

All Soviet children are indoctrinated in atheism and are expected to join young communist clubs when they begin school.

Here, a group of children at the Pioneer Palace dramatize the importance of safety rules.

Russian youth in modern western styles relax near the Neva River. Ancient church spires from Leningrad's Peter and Paul Fortress rise in the background.

Smiling Russian students buy "gazirovanaya voda,"
a flavored soda water, for a few kopecks
a glass from dispensing machines.

Like most Russian students, these boys
each carry a briefcase of homework and
wear a red scarf—the symbol of the Young
Pioneers communist club.

Workers barter produce at open-air markets—
the only official free enterprise.

Women work equally in most occupations with men—
a Soviet form of liberation.

Battalions of streetsweepers—mostly women—use hand-tied
twig brooms to keep Russian streets impressively clean.

СИЛЫ И ЗНАНИЯ
МОЛОДЫХ-ПЯТИЛЕТКЕ !

Propaganda posters abound across the vast Soviet
Union. This poster states that the growth and
education of youth is provided for in
five year work plans.

The slogan behind the statue of Lenin
proclaims, "Today Lenin is more alive
than all who live." Lenin has been
immortalized in countless ways.

Twenty million Russians died during World War II, leaving a shortage of men. Women, such as this road crew, shoulder much of the responsibility of labor.

A heroic statue depicts the emancipation of the Russian worker—from serf to citizen of the Union of Soviet Socialist Republics.

Russians listen avidly to Christian broadcasts from the West. Believers who cannot buy a Bible copy down Scripture read at dictation speed over the radio.

In a special church service, thankful Russian
Christians celebrate the fall harvest festival
with elaborate displays of fruit and vegetables.

Russian Christians write many of their own hymns.
In this church in central Russia, a group of
young Christians have organized their
own choir and orchestra.

Magnificent Orthodox churches, built during
the nine hundred years when Orthodoxy
was the official religion of Russia,
still stand.

The Soviets usually permit one Protestant
church to remain open in every city. Other Christians
meet in homes or in the forest.

wondering what the preparations entailed.

By this point in our travels inside the Soviet Union, we understood enough about Russia's vast system of watchers to be wary. "Don't ever say anything in your room you don't want monitored," a Christian woman who worked in a hotel in Odessa had once warned us. She, herself, had seen eavesdropping apparatus being installed in tourist rooms.

When we deposited our bags in room 205, Lena was sweeping the wooden floor in our room as rapidly as she could with a medieval type hand-tied twig broom that she dipped frequently in a murky pail of water.

Silver braided hair wreathed Lena's serene face. She straightened from her work and smiled when we came into the room. We spoke to her in Russian, but she only nodded her head, turned shyly back to her work, and then quickly left the room.

The next time we saw Lena, she was standing by the hotel elevator trying to calm an angry Russian guest. "But I tell you," the Russian's face flushed furiously, "this is the second time I have been stuck in that elevator. There is no excuse for this. That elevator should be fixed!" he huffed.

"*Nye rabotayet*—it's not working," Lena shrugged helplessly.

"Of course it's not working. It should be fixed!" the Russian guest bellowed.

Lena, bewildered how to mollify the man, led him to the stern woman at the front desk.

We followed along—curious how the indomitable clerk would answer this complaint. We had never been stuck in a Russian hotel elevator ourselves, but we had also never stayed in one hotel in the Soviet Union where all the elevators worked entirely. We frequently encountered elevators which could be used to go up or come down—but guests were often not permitted to ride both ways.

The irate guest marched after Lena to the main desk where he repeated his complaint to the unsmiling clerk. "*Tovarisch*—comrade," she spoke reproachfully, "the elevator works most of the time. Why are you complaining?"

The next day Lena timidly stopped Anita in the hall outside room 205. "*Eezvinitye*—forgive me," she murmured glancing over her shoulder as she spoke. "I wanted to ask you about that little book I saw on your table . . ."

Anita understood. Evidently we had left a booklet of the *Gospel of John* in Russian lying on the table beside our bed in the hotel room.

"Could you give me that little book?" Lena whispered.

"Do you want it now? Can you come with me?" Anita also kept her voice low.

Lena picked up her twig broom and slowly followed Anita down the hall as if she were coming to clean our room.

Inside Lena relaxed slightly when I switched on the radio to cover our conversation. However, she still spoke in a whisper.

"I am a Lutheran. I am a *verruyuscha*—a believer," Lena explained, "but I have no Bible."

"Is there a Lutheran Church here in the city?" I asked.

"It was closed," Lena shrugged sadly. "I do not know of any other churches."

The night before I had visited the only Protestant church in the city of N. I quickly copied the address and handed it to Lena. Gratefully she dropped the address in her apron pocket.

"Forty years ago I came from Finland to live in Leningrad," Lena said softly. "Then I had a Bible. Thirty years ago my Bible was destroyed in World War II during the siege of Leningrad."

Lena murmured the word "siege" with terror and momentarily all the fear of those days seemed to pass across her face.

A few days before in Leningrad we had met a taxi driver who had lived through the three years when Hitler's Nazi army attacked Leningrad and blockaded food supplies. Starvation ravaged the besieged city. Over five hundred thousand Leningraders died during those devastating nine hundred days. "Dead bodies were left to freeze in the streets like logs," the driver recalled with a shudder.

We told the driver we had read about the siege and that we understood why Leningrad is called a "hero city" of the Soviet Union. "Reading about it is not the same as living through it," the driver said tersely.

The three year siege had etched the taxi driver's mind with terrifying memories, but his spirit was soft and searching. He told me about his father who was a believer and had willed him a Bible.

"Do you ever listen to Christian broadcasts on short-wave radio?" I asked the driver.

He turned to face me in the back seat. "I not only listen but I have a great interest in the Christian broadcasts.

"Will you remember me—will you pray for me?" the taxi driver had pleaded as I stepped from his cab.

"I lived through the siege," Lena continued, "but my Bible was destroyed." She stared nervously at the door of our hotel room. "It is impossible to buy a Bible here in our country," she explained apologetically.

I quickly handed Lena a small Russian Bible I carried in my pocket. For a moment Lena caressed the cover with her calloused fingers. With simple sincerity she thanked us. Then she dropped the Bible in her capacious apron, lifted her broom and pail of water, and disappeared down the hall.

We didn't expect to see Lena again. But the next morning she slowly scrubbed the hall outside our room and waited for us. A beatific smile shone from her face. "I had to see you. I must thank you again for the precious

51

gift you gave me yesterday.

"For thirty years I have been praying for a Bible. I have had prayer and life is good when I pray, but now I have a Bible," she clasped her hands as if she cradled the Bible in them. "Last night I stayed up most of the night to read it."

Lena could not linger any longer in the hall by room 205. She plodded down the hall with her broom and bucket of water.

"I Believe in Man"

Olga, our Intourist guide in the city of V., reminded me of the Amazon women who lived along Russia's Don River during the reign of the Greeks. Even Alexander the Great was reputedly afraid to try to conquer them. According to legend, he feared that if he lost he would be forever ashamed to say he'd been defeated by women.

The first time we met Olga she wore white patent boots, a navy blue quilted coat, an oversized amber ring, and a charming smile. Her fair skin and reddish-blonde hair looked Scandinavian, but her statuesque size and slightly dominating attitude were Russian.

Although Olga traveled constantly across the Soviet Union as an Intourist guide, she was married and had a six-year-old daughter at home. She was proud of her husband, Alexsandr, a prominent Jewish scientist.

Even though Olga was devoted to her Jewish husband, she was curiously somewhat anti-Semitic. Once at lunch, an American tourist asked Olga about the exit tax the Soviet government levies against Russian Jews who want to emigrate.

"But any Jew can pay that exit tax," Olga lowered her voice confidentially. "The Jews are not like us. They are very, very rich. They belong to a privileged class," she summed up the situation denigratingly.

To prove her point, Olga told us an anecdote about Hiram, a Russian Jew who wanted to emigrate to Israel. "The Soviet government gave Hiram a permit to emigrate, but when he got to Israel he wasn't happy and wanted to return to the Soviet Union. So the Soviet government allowed him to return," Olga said, "but then Hiram decided he wanted to go back to Israel."

At this point, according to Olga's version of the story, the benevolent Soviet government mildly reproved the indecisive emigrant. "What's the matter, Hiram, don't you know your own mind? First you say you want to go to Israel and then you say you want to return to Russia."

Olga concluded her story with a hearty laugh. "Hiram told the authorities, 'I don't really want to live in Russia, and I don't really want to live in Israel. But I do like the stop-over in Vienna.'"

The following night Olga invited us to sit with her and her husband and two other tourists at the restaurant. We accepted enthusiastically—eager to meet her husband, Alexsandr.

Alexsandr, who had curly, black hair was husky, handsome, and slightly shorter than his wife, who that night at the restaurant wore her hair piled elegantly high on her head.

As often happened at an Intourist restaurant, a clamorous orchestra competed with our conversation. That night the orchestra played a haunting Jewish melody. A stocky woman singer in a blue uniform gripped the microphone and belted out the words in an unsmiling contralto voice. At the table, our conversation turned to the Jewish song and the subject of Jews in the Soviet Union.

"Are many Jews religious in the Soviet Union?" one of the American women asked Alexsandr. Somewhat condescendingly, Olga translated the question to her husband.

Alexsandr replied readily, "No—nobody believes here —either in God or the devil." He laughed, "If there is a God, I guess He'll punish us."

Olga translated Alexsandr's answer to us and then added her own explanation for emphasis. "Religion is just not an important subject in our country. It is dying out. There are almost no churches and only the old believe. There are no young people in the churches," she finished firmly.

Olga seemed mildly startled when we told her "there are many Christian young people in our country." We mentioned a major news article in *Time* magazine that reported on the "Jesus people."

Olga was unimpressed. "Our growing movement is Marxism and Leninism," she said emphatically.

"It is not that I am particularly antireligious," Olga explained more tolerantly, "but it is just that I can't believe in anything that I can't hold in my hands."

"Do you believe in love?" a Canadian tourist asked.

Olga considered the question. "My love for my child is biological. My love for my husband is sexual. It can all be explained in scientific terms. But I do believe in something," Olga stated conclusively, "I believe in man."

"But man's historical performance has not provided much basis for hope in humanism," the Canadian tourist observed.

Olga, who remembered the atrocities of World War II as a child, agreed that "man has made mistakes in the past," but she remained unmoved in her confidence that man could build a communist world—a new world.

"Man will perform properly if his environment is controlled. To control his environment, we must understand what Freud said about the makeup of man," she insisted.

While Olga talked with the Americans in English, I began to translate the conversation in Russian to Alexsandr who sat quietly at his wife's side.

"But it is impossible if you are intelligent to consider religion seriously," Alexsandr echoed his wife's objections. "There is no proof. Besides, no person who has studied science could become a Christian. Science and atheism are the same thing!"

"There are many scientists outside the Soviet Union who are Christians," I interposed. "They believe in God. They believe that only Christ can change a man."

Olga overheard our conversation. "Man doesn't need Christ," she said adamantly. "Man can change himself if he is directed properly. Our Soviet laws can change a man. We have moral codes in the Soviet Union," she boasted.

We talked for two hours more. By the end of our conversation, Olga still insisted that religion was "obsolete."

But what baffled me most that night about Olga was the tiny cross she wore around her neck. She said a tourist had given it to her.

"Don't Give It to Me Here"

Unlike the other purposeful citizens pushing by us on Leningrad's busy Nevsky Prospekt, one man was in no hurry. A stubby Russian with a painful limp, he slowed to a halt by the hedge where I stood cocking my camera to shoot a photo of the Museum of the History of Religion and Atheism.

"Enjoying your visit to Leningrad?" the man asked sociably when he saw my camera.

"Leningrad's a beautiful city," I replied.

"Well, it is a beautiful city." Relieved that I could speak Russian, the man continued the conversation. "You know, our city was almost destroyed in the war. *Slava Bogu*— thank God, we rebuilt it!" he said.

By now I was accustomed to the common expression *"slava Bogu*—thank God," an idiom which Russians, atheistic or otherwise, sprinkle freely throughout their conversation.

Nevertheless, I decided to explore the man's remark "Oh, you believe in God, do you?"

The man who had by now introduced himself as Gregor stared at me with surprise. "I—I'm not sure," he mused. "All I know about God is what I've seen in there." He motioned to the imposing Museum of the History of Religion and Atheism. "You been inside yet?" he asked.

Earlier, I had spent hours inside the museum, and I guessed what Gregori's impression would be if the museum were his only exposure to religion.

That morning, Anita and I had mingled with other sightseers inside the museum. I saw guides leading several groups of children through the massive marble pillars of the museum. They passed under a banner with a quotation from Marx which read, "The most important phase of eliminating religion lies in the education of children." A nearby quotation said, "Lenin's slogans are better than anything else for children."

A poster depicting four happy teenagers joining hands declared, "Communism is a young world with young people insuring its progress."

In one photo a young Russian couple exchanged wedding vows. The headline above them observed, "How fortunate it is for young people to be married in Soviet wedding palaces rather than churches."

A large scroll, unfurled over a buddha-like bust of Lenin, asserted, ". . . it is our duty to organize the widest possible intellectual and antireligious propaganda." One huge graph demonstrated the impressive climb in output of atheistic literature since the Bolshevik Revolution—over a thousand different titles and millions of books covering every aspect of atheism.

A painted display in the cathedral nave painstakingly traced the doctrine of the Trinity to pagan origins. A beautiful enamel mural depicting Russia's astronauts boasted, "From idols to the stars . . ."

"Yes," I said to Gregori, "I've been inside the museum, and I agree with some of their accusations against religion."

"But how can that be?" Gregori was bewildered. "Aren't you a *relighioznik*—a religious person?"

I told Gregori I was a *verruyuschiy*—a believer. "There is a big difference between being religious and being a follower of Jesus Christ," I explained as the crowds on Nevsky Prospekt pressed around us.

"But who is Jesus Christ?" Gregori puzzled. When I explained that Jesus is God's Son, Gregori was even more mystified.

"How could Jesus help a man like me?" Gregori stared at his twisted leg. "We could rebuild Leningrad, but what about me?" Gregori shifted his weight from his lame leg and almost painfully began to reminisce about his life. Born after the Bolshevik Revolution, he had been reared totally in communist ideology. Apart from the few times he had visited the Museum of Religion and Atheism, he knew nothing about Christianity or the Bible.

During World War II, Gregori was drafted into the Russian army. He fought in the brutal war against the "German fascists." He came out of the war alive, but crippled.

Gregori fondly remembered the Americans he had fought beside in the trenches of World War II. "I like Americans," he smiled, "but I never met one in the army who believed like you do in Jesus."

"I have a Bible I could give you," I said cautiously, "if you would like to read Jesus' words yourself."

"I sure would," Gregori said emphatically, not minding if he sounded eager. "But don't give the Bible to me here," he added quickly.

I understood. Nevsky Prospekt, Leningrad's busiest boulevard . . . in front of the Museum of Religion and Atheism . . . was not the most suitable place to offer a

Soviet citizen a Bible.

That morning an amusing—and revealing—incident had happened inside the museum which helped me appreciate Gregori's caution.

Anita and I were standing in a dimly lighted corridor of the museum studying a macabre painting of the Spanish inquisition. Suddenly I realized that four boys—about ten to twelve years old—were trailing us. They huddled together, whispering and glancing toward us. I guessed they wanted to ask us for gum.

When the corridor was deserted except for us and the band of boys, I turned and smiled at them. With a wink and jerk of his head, the oldest boy summoned me to the corner. The other boys stood like sentries ready to warn their leader if anyone approached.

"*Gospodeen*—Mister, could you give us some gum?" the leader whispered urgently. I slipped a package into his hand. Seeing the transaction was successful, another boy hissed, "Hide it."

The boys shoved a "*snachky*"—a small souvenir pin of Lenin into my hand to thank us. Then with amusing nonchalance, they strolled casually away—already masters of a system of subterfuge accepted by Soviet citizens as a normal inconvenience of life.

"Why don't we walk away from here—to the canal," I suggested to Gregori. He hobbled along beside us toward the changeless canal.

Half a block down the canal we stopped and gazed raptly into the placid water. I closed my hand around the small New Testament and slid my hand casually along the railing. Gregori rested his hand beside mine. His eyes steady on the canal before us, he slid the New Testament out from my hand to his.

"Is this in Russian?" he asked, still staring at the canal. I told him it was. He thanked me nervously. "Good-bye for now," he said. He turned and limped back toward Nevsky Prospekt.

Anita and I stayed at the railing watching the calm flowing waters of the canal.

THE CHRISTIANS

A Dangerous Book

The meeting was over. Believers slipped quietly down
the street from the Baptist Church in the city of B. We
caught up with two men from the congregation striding
toward the streetcar.

At first we spoke about the usual neutral topics of
weather and crops. Then when we were alone on the dark
street, the two men introduced themselves. The older man,
Steffan, was father-in-law to the younger, Vasily. They
were both leaders in the church. Vasily worked unofficially
with the young people. "We meet in different homes . . .
on week nights," he confided carefully.

If Vasily was leading Christian youth meetings, I understood his caution and admired his concern. I knew a little
about the Soviet government strictures against working
with young people—such as article 122 of the criminal
codex which makes "giving of religious instruction to
youth" an offense punishable by corrective labor.

I remembered three girls I had heard about in a church in southern Russia, who had organized a youth choir. For their efforts they were each sentenced to one year in a "lager"—a Russian work camp.

When I left the service that night, I noticed several people carrying square parcels wrapped in newsprint that I guessed were Bibles or hymn books. But Vasily, the youth leader, and his father-in-law were empty handed. Curious, I asked, "Do you have a Bible, Vasily Mikhailovich?"

Vasily glanced quickly behind us and replied, "No, I no longer have a Bible. At one time I did."

I wanted to hear Vasily's story, but we were almost to the cluster of people waiting for the street car and I supposed he would hesitate to talk. Hastily I spoke, "Would you like to have a Bible? It's at my hotel. Can you come part way with me?"

Under the glaring street lights, Vasily and his father-in-law exchanged amazed glances. They whispered excitely for a few minutes and then Vasily turned eagerly, "Pyotr Petrovich, I want a Bible at any cost. But how much shall I pay you for this Bible?"

"Nothing. The Bible is a gift from Christians in the West," was all I had time to whisper as the streetcar shuddered to the corner stop and we shoved on.

Inside the streetcar, the men discreetly paid no particular attention to me and didn't even talk much to each other. I knew, however, they were silently scheming how we could safely exchange the Bible.

I was grateful I had a Bible to give them. I thought back to the uncertain morning several days before when Anita and I had flown into Russia and how close we had come to not having a Bible to give the two Christian men now.

In the sturdy Soviet Aeroflot plane, we had lifted off from Prague at 8:20 a.m., our luggage loaded with Russian Bibles . . . so many Bibles that we knew we could not avoid their being easily evident to the searching eye of a customs official.

During the two hour flight from Prague to Moscow, we prayed. I'd been to Russia before. I knew that there are no recorded Soviet laws which prohibit bringing in Bibles as gifts. But I also knew that Bibles are likely to be arbitrarily confiscated at the Russian border by guards under atheistic orders. As the plane circled the airport, I thought of Christians in the U.S.S.R. who, I was certain, were praying and waiting for the Bibles we carried in our suitcases.

Inside the Moscow airport, scant lines formed in front of us at four customs counters. We chose a counter controlled by a woman official and stepped into line. A man in front of us haggled with the woman about the low rate of currency exchange.

"Not even one rouble for one dollar!" he exclaimed angrily. "In Austria they would have given me six of your roubles for one American dollar, and now you propose to give me 89 kopecks for one dollar? Not even one rouble?" he repeated sarcastically.

The woman, who wore a large Lenin souvenir pin on her lapel, inflexibly restated the rules. "You are not allowed to bring roubles into the Soviet Union. Money must be exchanged here—and at our rate of exchange." The man glared at the woman and shoved his American dollars across the counter.

Behind us a man was shouting into an uncooperative intercom, "I repeat—I am Ivan Andreyevich from the Academy of Sciences and I expected to be met here at the airport!"

The indifferent voice from the other squawked back, "Who are you? What do you want?"

The ignored personage from the Academy of Sciences, the highest academic body in the Soviet Union, shouted imperiously into the intercom, "I am Ivan Andreyevich and I demand . . ."

Then out of the collage of activity, it was suddenly our turn. The woman official, we noticed, had waved on the enraged passenger in front of us—without stopping to examine his luggage.

We shoved our Bible-loaded suitcases onto the counter and waited. She lifted one routinely, opened nothing, and turned to the money exchange forms. Almost unable to believe the miracle we prayed for had really happened, we whispered our thanks to God.

Now several days later, the streetcar shivered to a stop at the subway terminal and passengers emptied out onto the dully lighted street. The two men edged closer and the older one whispered, "We'll just wait here a few minutes, Pyotr Petrovich—wait until the others have gone on ahead. There were some who knew us on the streetcar."

Eventually, the other passengers disappeared down the steep subway stairs or melted off into the street. We waited for about fifteen minutes—speaking little until the subway terminal was crowded again with new passengers. Then we followed as the two men backtracked from the terminal down a somnolent street.

"It is best we take a different route," Steffan, the father-in-law explained briefly. "There are always informers at the church services." Vasily hurried a few blocks ahead to find a taxi.

Inside the taxi, Anita and I didn't talk at all. The driver was listening. We knew our Russian had an American accent and we didn't want our Russian friends to have to explain why they were accompanied by two foreigners.

We stopped two blocks from the hotel near a busy subway entrance. As the two men had planned, we were surprisingly swallowed in the swirling crowd of commuters at the subway stop. We leaned into the shadows beneath a long Lenin mural.

It was reasonably safe to talk again, and I asked Vasily what had happened to his first Bible. "The Bible I once had," he reminisced, "I bought from a friend who found it in an attic. My friend was not a believer and was happy to sell the Bible.

"Since the Bible was old and falling apart, my friend only charged fifty roubles."

Fifty roubles, I knew, was equivalent to one half month's wages for Vasily. But he did not seem dismayed at the exorbitant price. In fact he told the story as if he had found a bargain.

I knew that the Soviet government has allowed only token printings of Scriptures—about thirty thousand Bibles for Evangelical Christians in the last forty-five years.

I also knew that Russian Christians cannot buy a Bible or a Christian book in any bookstore in their very literate country. I understood why Vasily was willing to pay half a month's wages for a Bible.

"The worn Bible I bought from my friend . . . well, I gave that Bible away." Vasily continued almost apologetically.

Proud of his new possession, he had taken the Bible home to show his father, who lived in the country. When the father saw his son's treasure, he begged him for the Bible. "Here in the village, there is little hope of ever finding a Bible. In the city you might some day find another one," his father reasoned.

"I knew my father really needed a Bible," Vasily said. "He hadn't had a Bible for years. In fact, there was no Bible in the entire village, so I gave him mine. That was five years ago.

"I know I made the right choice though," Vasily reflected earnestly. "My father started inviting neighbors in to read the Scriptures to them. Since he's had the Bible, several of the villagers have accepted Christ. The Bible has brought fruit."

I had hurried to church that night and had forgotten to carry a Russian Bible with me as I usually did. I explained

71

to the men that the Bibles were locked in my hotel room. "We'll wait here," they smiled.

Inside the hotel, I stowed a Bible inside my pocket. Anita was wearing a bright green coat which she insisted was old and worn. By Soviet standards, however, it looked distractingly bright. She changed to a gray plastic raincoat and we strolled down the street to where our friends waited.

As we walked, Vasily stepped out of the darkness and walked beside us. I slipped him the Bible. "Thank you, Brother, for this *'choodiny podarok*—wonderful gift,' " he said warmly. As is the custom among Russian Christians, Vasily kissed me. Then he faded into the darkness.

There was no formal good-bye or greeting . . . no exchange of addresses or plans to correspond in the future. But I understood. I was in Russia—not just another country, but in another world . . . a world where a Bible is considered a dangerous book.

"We're Not Hiding Anything"

We slogged through the night up the muddy road to Mikhail and Anna's house. In the dark the furious rain seemed to be washing ravines in the already rutted road.

We had originally met Mikhail and Anna three years ago at a Russian church in the city of R. They told us they listened every day to the Christian broadcasts from missionary stations outside their country, and insisted we come visit them at their home if we ever returned to the city of R.

Through the black night we finally found their house gate and pressed the buzzer. Mikhail pried open the gate to peek out. When he recognized us, he threw the gate open and flung his arms about us. We followed him past the tiny courtyard striped with rows of flowers and vegetables into his tiny cottage.

Anna hugged us into her small house and urged us toward the living room. She guided us past a small curtained cubicle that was the kitchen. A bathtub stood in one corner of the room.

The cottage—which consisted of a kitchen, dining room, living room, and a tiny bedroom—was austere but clean and homey. A wooden buffet, one of the scarce pieces of furniture which stood in the dining room, held so few dishes it looked as if someone were playing house.

Anna guided us on tiptoe past the dining room where Fanya, the youngest child, lay swathed in a heavy quilt on a couch that was used as a bed.

In the living room, bleached embroidered doilies decorated the sofa. A flourishing green plant as tall as a small tree stood in the center of the room. The two older children, Katya and Yakov, hung shyly in the living room door while we spoke softly with their parents.

Proudly Anna showed us a bayan, an accordion-like instrument lying on a chair in the living room. "Yakov and Katya have started to take lessons from a sister at the church. They want to play in the church orchestra," she explained.

When we asked about her health, Anna evaded our questions. From our last visit we knew she had heart trouble, but still worked as a nurse in a kindergarten school to help support her family.

"*Neechevo*—it is nothing. It is all right," she shrugged. "We are able to work and live and we have plenty to eat. And God has helped us finish our cottage. Now we can have meetings here," she said happily.

Before we left that evening, Mikhail and Anna decided they must tell the other believers we had come. A meeting was hastily planned for the following night in their cottage.

Surprisingly, Anna quickly packed a black overnight satchel for Mikhail and pressed a handkerchief into his hand. "I'll go tonight to tell the others you've come. When I finish, it will be morning," he explained simply.

As we left the cottage, we heard Anna admonishing the two older children, "You are wise children. You know that we must not mention that our aunty and uncle came to visit . . ."

The next night we walked again past the cabbage plants, rose bushes, and sunflower stalks into Mikhail and Anna's spotlessly clean cottage.

"In case anyone should ask, we are celebrating Marina's fortieth birthday," Anna gestured to a smiling woman who looked at least fifty.

As part of the celebration, which was an "excuse" for a Christian meeting, Anna had prepared a robust Russian meal. Monstrous plates of mashed potatoes, boiled duck, tomatoes, and mounds of fresh fruit were set before us.

Relentlessly the Russians urged us to eat. "You look so small—so sickly," they worried over Anita. "Is it really true," a stout woman chuckled, "that you Americans keep scales just to weigh on in your homes?"

Cut off by their country's censorship, the Christians were starved for news of Christianity in the West. In their own Soviet press, they had read only that Christianity was dying everywhere.

Through adverse reports in their newspapers, they all knew about Billy Graham whom, in spite of their media, they greatly admired. However, they had difficulty comprehending a government that would permit a preacher to conduct huge evangelistic campaigns or speak to millions by television. "The Apostle Paul must envy Billy Graham," one bearded lay preacher mumbled wistfully.

We later smiled at a difficulty the believers had with a recent press item. One of the Russians had read in the Soviet press that Billy Graham was indecently accompanied on a recent evangelistic trip by a woman singer— "a certain Beverly Shea." The Christians were greatly relieved when I told them that was *George* Beverly Shea, the male soloist of the Billy Graham team.

The Christians questioned me closely about missionary work conducted from the West—a concept they, who have no missionary organizations, found mystifying. "Your government permits a Christian citizen to live in another country to preach?" They were incredulous.

"But who pays for it?" they persisted.

"In our country, every Christian is a missionary," one of the men summed up the difference.

When I questioned the Russians about their church life, I was impressed by their lack of complaint at restrictions most Western Christians would consider impossible. Several of the believers conceded that their life was difficult —*trudno*."

"But the Christians in China . . . their situation is *ochen trudno*—very difficult!" one of the men exclaimed. "We must pray for our brothers and sisters there."

"Do you meet often in homes for church services?" I asked.

"In our town we do have a registered church," one of the men explained. "Many of us attend there. But it is not large enough to contain all the Christians who want to worship. So sometimes we must meet in homes or in the woods."

"Some of us refuse to attend the registered church," a man across the room added firmly. "We left the church in 1961 when our government sent out 'rules of instruction' to all churches belonging to the AUCECB (All Union Council of Evangelical Christians and Baptists). These rules denied our children the right to attend church. The government also said we could not openly conduct youth meetings. The rules interfered unconstitutionally with our church life."

"Now there are Christians like us meeting in thousands of homes all over the Soviet Union," Mikhail explained, and the others shook their heads in agreement.

"The government does not approve of house meetings,"

77

Anna sighed wearily, "but they will not give us a permit to register officially so that we can have enough church buildings. We are forced to meet without their approval."

I asked the Christians if they referred to their meetings outside the registered churches as underground meetings—a term often used in the West. "We're not hiding anything. We do not want to be underground!" they were indignant. "We only ask to worship openly as our Soviet constitution says we have a legal right to do."

"Does the government know you are meeting?"

"*Konechno*—of course!" several of the Christians exclaimed at once. "There are eyes everywhere! The government knows everything. Sometimes they let us meet without disruption. Other times," the spokesman's face grew somber, "they fine us. Some Christians are sitting in prison now for conducting Sunday school meetings in their homes."

Mikhail had not been fined for the meetings he held regularly in his home, but he knew another group of believers meeting in a home who had. "The police came and fined the owner of the house fifty roubles," Mikhail explained. The Christians took an offering, paid the police the fifty roubles, and continued the meeting."

Nobody announced that the meeting was over at Anna and Mikhail's house, but as quietly as they had come, the Christians slipped away into the courtyard.

We said good-bye to Anna and Mikhail and they shoved two unwieldy watermelons into our arms. Anna insisted we must take them. "It is a gift from our house meeting," she said. But the real gift was the expression of love in her eyes.

If One of Us Is Taken

"*Nyet—nyet.* There is no Baptist Church in this city," the clerk at the Intourist desk insisted strenuously when I asked for directions to the Baptist Church—the only Protestant church in the city of K.

Despite the clerk's denial, I knew there was a church in the city of K. because I had visited there three years before—but forgotten the address. Now, realizing that directions from Intourist were unlikely, I set out to retrace my steps.

I finally found the right street, but could not find number 39—the church address. I approached an old man ambling aimlessly up the street. "I'll show you myself," he replied helpfully, switching directions when I asked for advice.

"So you are a stranger in our town," he speculated. "What part of the country are you from?" He seemed honestly surprised when I admitted I was not a Russian citizen, but an American.

"An American!" he exclaimed. He halted in the street and spoke stealthily, "Is it really true? Is it better there?" From that point, the curious old man slowed his steps to prolong the pleasure of talking to someone from "outside."

Finally we reached a peeling gray gate with the number 39 hung uncertainly from the front. Inside the muddy courtyard, huts decorated with fretwork design clung to the sloping wood fence. The church, its majestic blue Orthodox dome thrust to the sky, stood on the far side of the courtyard. Low strains of exultant hymns radiated from the church out to the courtyard.

Inside the church the choir was practicing, but the service hadn't started. From my visit three years before, I remembered that the preachers met before the service in a small room behind the church.

I knocked at the door. "Brother Pyotr!" Sergei, a preacher with a bristling black beard whom I had met three years ago engulfed me in a Russian embrace. He hospitably introduced us to the twelve other preachers— all of whom wore suits and Sunday shirts, without neckties.

I remembered several of the preachers from my visits three years before. I knew there were at least fifteen lay pastors in the church in K., an arrangement typical of Protestant churches in Russia. Once a lay pastor had explained to me, "If one of us is taken, others can step in."

"First, Brother Pyotr, tell us if you have brought any gifts," Sergei, the preacher with the beard, beamed. I knew Sergei meant Bibles. That morning before we left the hotel, Anita had placed four New Testaments and a small Bible concordance inside her deep purse. The preachers watched eagerly as she dug inside the handbag.

With awe the men reached for the books. It was then I noticed the blind preacher. He sat silently on a bench staring nowhere. Gently one of the preachers guided the blind man's hand to the New Testament. The blind preacher lovingly traced the cover of the book he could not read.

"You remembered us," one of the preachers spoke through the silence. "Twenty believers were baptized in our church this summer and we had almost nothing to give them. But now we have Bread—and the concordance! Today we are rich men. Let us stand, pray, and thank God, brethren!" the preacher said jubilantly.

Unlike the old man I had met that morning on the way to church, the preachers were not interested in living conditions in America. But they were eager for news of the Church in the West.

"Why are there so many different groups of Christians in America?" The preachers, accustomed to one official church, were baffled by the proliferation of denominations in America.

"How many preachers do you have speak at each meeting? How long are your meetings?" The preachers shook their heads disapprovingly at the thought of an American service that had only one preacher and lasted only one hour.

One of the preachers told me about a meeting in a nearby village where he had preached two weeks before. "There were eight preachers and the meeting lasted five hours."

Ceremoniously, the preachers asked me to carry their *"preeveti*—greetings—back to our brothers and sisters in America." The preachers were particularly thankful for Christians in the West whom they knew helped support the Gospel programs broadcast to the Soviet Union from missionary stations.

"They haven't forgotten us," one preacher said.

"I hope you and the other radio speakers don't mind," Sergei declared apologetically, "but we pastors copy the outlines from the sermons we hear on the radio. Then we preach them to our congregation. The broadcasts are our seminary," he explained.

A young preacher who had been sitting silently on a bench by the door turned toward me. "I am today a preacher because of your broadcasts, Pyotr Petrovich," he said slowly, and the small room grew silent while the preacher, whose name was Igor, told me his story.

Four years before, Igor had been tinkering with his shortwave radio when he discovered a Christian broadcast from the missionary station HCJB in Quito, Ecuador.

"At that time I was 33 years old and an atheist," Igor said, "but I was intrigued by the speaker who talked about God as if He really existed."

Igor listened to the broadcasts for almost a year. One day in January—to the anger of his wife—he announced to his family that he had become a *"verruyuschiy*—a believer."

Igor's wife was furious at her husband's conversion, but she did notice his increased compassion toward his family. Furtively, she began to listen to the shortwave broadcasts herself.

After his conversion, Igor, who had never met a Christian before, wanted to meet other believers. But he had no idea where to find a church in his city. "I prayed like Cornelius in the *Book of Acts,*" Igor smiled. "God sent a believer to me who took me to the only Protestant church in our city."

Igor wanted to become a preacher, but he had no Bible nor any hope of attending a seminary, since the Soviet government does not allow Protestant Bible schools or seminaries to operate inside the U.S.S.R. Soon the shortwave broadcasts which had stimulated Igor's conversion also became a source of seminary training for the young Christian.

"Six months ago, the *bratya*—brothers here at the church appointed me to preach," Igor happily concluded.

By the time Igor finished his story, it was already past

83

time for the service to begin. I watched with interest as an older pastor selected four men, including Igor and the blind preacher, from among the twelve to preach that morning. From past experience in Russian churches, I knew that usually every pastor comes prepared to preach for every service and doesn't know who will be chosen.

Anita and I sat on the platform with the preachers who had asked me to bring "greetings," which I knew meant they wanted me to preach a short sermon to the congregation, who were pushed to the edge of the pulpit and crowded back to the walls of the church.

The church building, which was once an Orthodox church, had been allocated by the Soviet Department of Cults to the Baptists. Inside the impressive sanctuary a thin layer of blue paint coated the intricate icons.

Now plaques with portions of Scripture decorated the walls. But the Bible verses were more than a decorative replacement. Most of the Russian worshipers that morning carried no Bible.

When it was Igor's turn to preach, he pointed at the Scripture texts hanging on the wall. "Even you little babushkas who can't read," he exhorted, "when you get to Heaven—then you will know all of God's truths."

After the service, the congregation surrounded us to thank us for the Christian broadcasts. A heavy woman balanced on crutches wobbled toward us. She reached beyond her crutches and wrapped Anita in her arms. "*Syestra, spaceebo*—thank you, sister," she whispered. "Thank you for the broadcasts," she wept. "The radio missionaries are like my family."

Sergei, Igor and the other preachers insisted on escorting us to the trolley. On a street corner near the trolley stop, a gypsy was selling magnificent bouquets of gladiolus. Igor bought a bouquet and handed the flowers to Anita. "From all to us," he said simply.

"I Wouldn't Trade That Bible for a Thousand Roubles"

At noon we were the only customers in the Intourist hotel restaurant in the Ukrainian city of L. A plump waitress lingered in the kitchen door and a band practiced lethargically in the balcony above the dining room. At 12:15 another customer, a middle-aged Russian man, diffidently opened the door into the dining room.

The waitress noticed the man's timidity and ushered him to our table. "Do you mind if I sit here?" he hesitated.

"You're welcome," I replied warmly, hopeful for an opportunity to get acquainted.

We introduced ourselves and the Russian fixed his eyes on the listless band in the balcony overhead. Then—in an apparent reference to the dance band and the devastating drinking that occurred each evening at the Intourist restaurant—the man mumbled something about his "concern for the young people at the hotel."

"You know we have a saying here in Russia," the

Russian who had introduced himself as Ivan continued softly. "People who don't fear God have problems."

I was startled by this statement and decided to pursue the conversation. "Well," I replied speaking in Russian, "I do fear God. I'm a Christian."

"A *verruyuschiy*—a Christian!" Ivan's eyes shone. He clasped his hands in quiet joy and for the first time since we had met him he seemed to shed some of his fear.

But not for long. In seconds, he was again glancing apprehensively around the almost empty restaurant. He spoke cautiously—careful that the waitress would not overhear.

Happily no one sat near us and for about twenty minutes we were undisturbed except for infrequent intrusions by the indifferent waitress. Whenever the waitress did pause at our table, Ivan smoothly changed the conversation from the topic of Christianity. "How did we like the Ukrainian borscht? Would Anita have another *bulochka*—bun?"

Eventually the waitress began to take more interest in our table. Ivan fidgeted nervously, "You go down the stairs, up the street to the left into the park, Pyotr Petrovich," he said surreptitiously. "There we can walk and talk all we want."

Ivan and I left the hotel separately and met in the spacious park sculptured with acres of weedless flower gardens. We strolled past three gnarled grandmothers in dark cotton dresses and high boots who were tenderly transplanting peonies. While we walked, Ivan told me his story.

He lived in a village 200 kilometers away, and he had been sent by his factory who had paid for him to stay at the Intourist hotel while he did some business for them in the city of L.

Before Ivan moved to the town 200 kilometers from the city of L., he had lived in Komsomol, Siberia. This

Siberian town, which had been hewed out of the taiga by pioneering young communists, was as militant as the Komsomol (Young Communist League) in whose honor it was named.

There was no church in Komsomol. The city's founding fathers had determined that Komsomol, with its exemplary ideological heritage, must be totally communistic.

In Komsomol, Siberia, Ivan and his family felt isolated. Gospel broadcasts from a missionary station, HLKX in South Korea, were their only source of spiritual encouragement.

Eventually, Ivan began to hold Christian meetings in his home. At first his wife and four children comprised the only congregation, but then the meetings grew. Several people were converted and Ivan's tiny Siberian house could scarcely hold the crowd that met in the city of Komsomol to worship God.

Officials at Ivan's factory heard about the expanding meetings. At first Ivan was warned to stop. When the gatherings continued, Ivan—whose industrious record at the factory was irreproachable—was fired. When he tried to apply for other jobs, he discovered that a file documenting his Christian activities had been sent ahead.

"But I did not let the matter rest there." To my surprise, Ivan explained how he had written to Moscow to complain. "By this time we had seven children," he said simply. "I had no way to feed them."

Ivan wrote a Moscow official in charge of labor. He reminded the official that when he had applied for the factory job in the city of Komsomol, nobody asked if he were a believer. But when his religious convictions (a right theoretically protected by article 124 of the Soviet constitution) were discovered, he was dismissed from his job.

Nineteen days after he wrote his letter—when his family had already been three days without food—officials from the factory in Komsomol reinstated Ivan in his job.

Even during the time he was without a job, Ivan had not stopped the Christian meetings in his home. As a result of his determined witness, today there is a church in Komsomol.

Later Ivan and his family moved five thousand miles across Siberia to European Russia, to the town where he now lived. They were welcomed by the small band of believers in this town of eighteen hundred people.

In the last few years, the church in Ivan's town had flourished. "Now there are almost six hundred Christians in our town," he smiled. "The authorities call our town the City of God! Christianity is spreading so fast where I live that the authorities say it is a 'contagious disease.' They have even tried to quarantine our town.

"The authorities refuse to give residence permits to new citizens. They are afraid if nonbelievers live among us they will become converted to Christ! The authorities are especially cautious about the police assigned to patrol Christian gatherings. They try to transfer them every few months."

Ivan and I wandered near a park bench overhung by drooping poplar trees. We sat down and I asked Ivan to tell me more about the fiery church in the "City of God."

But by this time Ivan had discovered that I sometimes spoke on the Christian broadcasts and knew the other radio missionaries. He stammered excitedly, "You know, I've got questions to ask you up to here," he gestured to his forehead. "There is so much we do not know, and we have so few Bibles and no Christian books."

For an hour we sat talking on the secluded bench. Ivan asked questions about Christian living—questions about Scriptures he did not understand. What was the unpardonable sin? Was divorce ever allowable for a Christian? Can a Christian ever be lost? How do events in Israel fit into Biblical prophecy?

We had only begun to discuss Ivan's barrage of questions, when a man with a newspaper strode purposefully in our direction and sat on our short bench—ignoring the other empty benches scattered about the park.

The man unrolled his newspaper but did not read. He first studied my western wing-tipped shoes. Then he ostensibly started to read the newspaper—and not too subtly—waited for us to continue our conversation.

Ivan immediately switched the subject. We discussed that year's bumper crop in the Ukraine, and then Ivan casually announced, *"Nu, mnye nuzhno eetee*—well, I guess I must be going." Discreetly, I drifted off in the opposite direction.

The next morning Ivan waited for me outside the hotel. "Before I go home, Pyotr Petrovich," he said, "I must tell you the story of my daughter, Tanya."

Tanya was born when Ivan and his wife lived in the city of Komsomol in Siberia. As a child, she clung to her parents and their faith while her family was battered for its Christian witness.

Then the family had moved to western Russia. By this time Tanya was a teenager, and like all Soviet young people, her teachers pressured her to join the atheistic Komsomol youth club—the only gateway for a Soviet young person to academic, social, and job success.

Against her parents' advice and her own earlier Christian commitment, Tanya joined the Komsomol and fiercely dedicated her life to communism. Her dedication was so total that her parents worried their own daughter might betray them.

Recently, Tanya had moved to her older brother's house in another city so she could attend the university there. She avoided her brother and his wife, who were believers, when they prayed or talked about God. But secretly, Tanya started to listen to the Christian broadcasts on her brother's shortwave radio.

"And the Lord, Himself, spoke to Tanya through that radio!" Ivan told me with joy in his eyes. "Seven months ago, I received a telegram from my son. The telegram said simply, 'February 18 Tanya was born.' My son knew I would understand. On that day Tanya was born again."

As we strolled through the glistening park, neither of us spoke—the father moved by the miracle of his daughter's conversion. I was awed at the mercy of God who uses men and their inventions to speak His glory.

"When you return to the West, thank the Christians who sent the broadcasts," Ivan broke the silence.

"In six months my Tanya will be baptized. She is begging me for a Bible. I have a Bible myself but I must keep it for the meetings," Ivan sighed heavily.

I had one Russian Bible left. It was in my hotel room and I quickly resolved that God had preserved it until this point in our trip for me to give to Ivan for his daughter.

Ivan had to leave the hotel for home in one hour. I knew it would not be discreet for us to meet again within sight of the watchful hotel doorman or the woman guard whom I had seen faithfully recording comings and goings of hotel guests.

A long staircase with an elevator in the center spiraled from our floor down to the hotel restaurant. "Behind the elevator shaft—meet me there in thirty minutes," I whispered as we parted near the hotel door.

Casually, Anita and I wandered down the staircase. Ivan slowly caught up with us. I slipped him the Bible for Tanya and a hymn book for his wife whom he had told me liked to sing.

He clutched the books in his hands. "I wouldn't trade that Bible for a thousand roubles, Pyotr Petrovich. And the hymn book—my wife will sing praises to God the rest of her life!"

The More People Know

"You leave it to me if the authorities ask any questions!" Fyodr said firmly when I suggested that maybe we would cause problems for him if we visited his apartment.

"You are my dear guests from the West, and I am inviting you home to dinner," the stocky, determined Russian repeated immovably.

I had met Fyodr in a church service in the town of S. After the three hour service, Fyodr insisted that Anita and I come to his house for lunch.

We turned the corner to Fyodr's apartment and confronted an unshaven Russian worker who held a bottle of vodka in one hand. With his other hand he gently rocked a buggy with a sleeping baby inside bundled in fluffy white quilts. Fyodr passed his neighbor with a nod and we marched on through the cement corridor to his apartment.

Three pairs of small polished shoes stood in a neat row by the entry door. Inside the apartment, Fyodr's three children played in stocking feet on the painted, wood floor. Fyodr's wife, Irina, a nurse, was scrubbing potatoes. One by one she dropped the huge heap into a kettle of boiling water.

Fyodr motioned me to a chair. He glanced out the window and pulled the curtains on the already shaded room before he sat down himself.

Fyodr worked in a factory where tractor parts were assembled. "The foreman at the factory knows I am a *verruyuschiy*—a believer," Fyodr stated simply. "We often have lectures on atheism at the factory. The foreman ridicules me, but I don't mind. I figure that everybody at the factory knows I'm a Christian by now. The ones who are searching for God know they can come to me for help."

Fyodr told us about one time when an atheistic agitator had been assigned to work beside him at the factory and persuade him to renounce his faith. Later the agitator confided to Fyodr that before he received his assignment he had been warned by the factory manager. "Don't let it happen to you as it did to that last worker I sent to change Fyodr. The last agitator became a Christian."

"The Bible says a believer must witness about his faith," Fyodr said resolutely. He motioned to the window sill where a few minutes before he had drawn the yellowed lace curtains. "In summertime," he explained, "I set my shortwave radio in the open window. I tune the radio to the Gospel broadcasts from Ecuador or Monte Carlo and I turn the volume high. People walking by on the sidewalk stop to listen under my window."

Fyodr belonged to the Baptist Church—the one Protestant group of believers in the city who had received permission to register. But Fyodr's church had suffered. "The government registered the church, but then they appointed one of the pastors," he explained. "The pastor was a back-slidden Christian who had turned to informing for the KGB.

"The whole church grieved. For awhile it seemed as if the Spirit of God had departed from our congregation, but we refused to let the government control our church," Fyodr hunched firmly forward as he continued his story.

"The real Christians of the church prayed. We prayed like the believers in the *Book of Acts* until 'the building shook.' The informer died, and now more people are coming to Christ in our church than ever before."

"What can Christians in the West do to help the church in Russia?" I questioned Fyodr when we sat at the dinner table drinking our glasses of hot tea.

"You can pray for us—and you can come visit us and encourage us," he smiled. His voice sobered, "But you must continue sending the broadcasts and bringing in literature. There is no other way, Pyotr Petrovich, for us to have this spiritual food."

Fyodr waited until Irina carried dishes from the room and the children were away from the table playing on the painted floor. Outside in the hall the baby awoke and wailed. The crying carried through the thin walls of Fyodr's apartment.

"There is one more thing you can do, Pyotr Petrovich," his voice fell to a whisper. He leaned toward me, "Tell the Christians in the West about our victories and our problems as believers here in the Soviet Union. The more people know there—the easier it is for us here."

This book is a compilation of true encounters with Russians that the authors experienced during their extensive travels inside the Soviet Union.

Although the experiences are true, the names of people have been changed and the names of cities abbreviated to protect the Russian citizens described in the book.

Peter and Anita Deyneka, Jr., are missionaries of the Slavic Gospel Association. Mr. Deyneka is also Associate Director of this mission, which sponsors 125 missionaries in 22 countries.

The SGA mission is responsible for several hundred Christian radio broadcasts transmitted each month to the U.S.S.R. This mission also delivers Bibles and Christian literature into the communist countries.

Slavic Gospel Association
2434 North Kedzie Blvd.
Chicago, IL 60647